Adopted and Loved Forever

Adopted and Loved Forever

by Annetta E. Dellinger
Pictures by Patricia Mattozzi

CONCORDIA

Publishing House
St. Louis

Dedicated to my goddaughter, Lisa Renee Burns, and my many friends who have been adopted by loving families and by their best Friend, their heavenly Father.

I have loved you with an everlasting love. (Jer. 31:3)

Special thanks to Rev. Ken Albers, Rev. Phill Andreasen, Carol Christene Dellinger, and Karen Boerger.

The Scripture quotations in this publication are from the Revised Standard Version of the Bible, copyrighted 1946, 1952 © 1971, 1973. Used by permission.

Copyright © 1987 Concordia Publishing House
3558 S. Jefferson Avenue, St. Louis, MO 63118-3968
Manufactured in the United States of America

Library of Congress Cataloging in Publication Data

Dellinger, Annetta E.
        Adopted and loved forever.

        Summary: A young child describes what it means to be adopted emphasizing that parents of adopted children chose them, love them, and will never leave them.
        1. Children, Adopted—Religious life. [1. Adoption. 2. Christian life] I. Title.
BV4571.2.D44   1987   248.8'2   86-32770
ISBN 0-570-04167-8

    2   3   4   5   6   7   8   9   10   PP   96   95   94   93   92   91   90   89

My parents are very special people, and I'm glad they're my parents. Mom and Dad were excited and happy when they adopted me and God made us a family. They love to give me hugs and tell me how special I am to them. I love them too!

My parents were lonely before they adopted me because they had no children to care for and love. They went to talk to a lady at the adoption agency. The agency knows where there are children who need families. The agency knew about me—and my parents chose me to be their child.

Now they aren't lonely any more, and neither am I. They have told me many times that the day I came to live with them was one of the happiest days of their lives. And mine, too!

My mother has soft, long blond hair and light blue eyes. She's not very tall. She has a dimple in her chin and likes to smile a lot. We have a lot of fun baking cookies together. She likes to put a little dab of flour on my chin to make it look like it has a dimple like hers. I think that's funny. When she hugs me, I feel warm and tingly inside because I know she loves me very, very much.

My daddy is tall. He has brown curly hair, dark brown eyes and wears glasses. I like the way he wrestles with me and tickles me. He has the funniest laugh! I can tell he's proud of me and that I am very special to him because he likes to have me do things with him. He says we're pals.

I don't look like either of my parents like some adopted children do, but that's okay. God made each of us different, and we're His special people.

Although I'm adopted, my parents still have me do things. Just like other kid's parents, they ask me to eat good foods, like spinach—yuk—and clean up my plate, brush my teeth, and pick up the toys.

They correct me when there's a need for it. I know they are helping me grow up. It's hard to know what's right and wrong when you are little. I think that's why God gave me parents. It makes me feel good to know that both Jesus and my parents forgive me.

Being part of a family—that's what "adopted" means to me. And I like being part of this family. Although my natural parents are the ones who brought me into this world, my adoptive parents are the people I call Mom and Dad. They are the people who take care of me and love me. I try to show Jesus how happy I am for giving me my mom and dad by obeying them and by showing them how much I love them.

Daddy says that lots of kids are adopted. In fact, some of my friends at Sunday school and church are adopted, too. Their names are Libby, Lisa, and Jeff. Lisa was adopted when she was 2, Libby when she was 8, and Jeff when he was 4. I was adopted when I was a tiny baby.

Mommy tells me there are many different reasons why children need adoptive families. Their natural parents might have died, or maybe the parents didn't have enough money to buy food and clothing and they knew there were other adults who could care for their child.

Sometimes I wonder if my mom and dad will still want me when I'm 10 or 12, or when I do something wrong or hurt their feelings. But they tell me to never worry about that because adoption is forever. God brought us together, and we are a family—no matter what happens. I like that!

I like to do things with my family, like going on picnics and bike riding, but I like it best when we all sit close together and Daddy reads the Bible for devotions. I like to hear that we are all God's children and part of His family.

Daddy reads God's words, "You did not choose me, but I chose you . . . " (John 15:16).

"Wow, God chose me!"

Then Daddy says that God not only chose us, He adopted us into His family (Gal. 4:5). God wants me in His heavenly kingdom just as my parents want me in their home.

Dad tells me that God thought about me long before I was ever born. He knows everything about me—when I stand up, sit down, and even how many hairs are on my head! I must really be important to Him!

After Daddy finishes reading the Bible, I look at Mommy and ask, "Please, just one more time, tell me about Esther in the Bible."

Mommy winks at me and pats me on the hand as she begins to read one of my favorite stories. Esther "had neither father nor mother, the maiden was beautiful and lovely, and when her father and her mother died, Mordecai adopted her as his own daughter" (Esther 2:7).

God took good care of Esther because He loved her. She was blessed to have Mordecai to love and care for her.

God is taking care of me, too, because He loves me very much. Being an adopted child is special. It means having parents who really love me and want me very much. I sure feel loved, and I hope Mom and Dad know I love them too!

Dear heavenly Father,

Thank You for giving me such a special family to be loved by and to live with. And, thank You for helping them teach me about Jesus, my Savior. I couldn't have chosen better parents. I don't always understand everything about being adopted, but that's okay, because I know that You love me and are caring for me through my parents. Help me to show my parents how much I love them for wanting me. And Father, I love You, too . . . very much. Amen.

I have loved you with an everlasting love.

(Jer. 31:3)